DOVER · THRIFT · EDITIONS

"God's Grandeur"
and Other Poems

GERARD MANLEY HOPKINS

DOVER PUBLICATIONS, INC.
New York

DOVER THRIFT EDITIONS

General Editor: Stanley Appelbaum
Editor of This Volume: Thomas Crofts

Bibliographical Note

This Dover edition, first published in 1995, is an unabridged republication of the poems from *Poems of Gerard Manley Hopkins* (Robert Bridges, ed.), Humphrey Milford, London, 1918. A new introductory Note, a set of explanatory end-notes and an Index of Titles and First Lines have been specially prepared for the present edition.

Library of Congress Cataloging-in-Publication Data

Hopkins, Gerard Manley, 1844–1889.
    [Poems]
    "God's grandeur" and other poems / Gerard Manley Hopkins.
      p.   cm.
    Originally published: Poems of Gerard Manley Hopkins. London : H. Milford, 1918.
    Includes index.
    ISBN 0-486-28729-7 (pbk.)
    I. Title.
PR4803.H44A17   1995
821'.8—dc20
                                      95-7154
                                       CIP

Manufactured in the United States of America
Dover Publications, Inc., 31 East 2nd Street, Mineola, N.Y. 11501

Note

The Jesuit priest and gifted classical scholar Gerard Manley Hopkins (1844–1889) was, with Browning, Tennyson and Arnold, one of the geniuses of nineteenth-century English poetry. Unlike his illustrious contemporaries, however, Hopkins was, in his lifetime, almost totally obscure, sharing his poetry only with a few intimate correspondents, and never seeking publication for his work. After taking holy orders in 1868 (just two years after an anguished conversion from his family's High Anglicanism) he burned his poems and committed himself to literary silence, feeling that aesthetic pursuits were inappropriate to his vocation. This was to become one of the great paradoxes of his life and religion, for, to Hopkins, that individuality of an artist or subject which comes through in a work of art is precisely the stuff of our spirit, our individual gift from God; he called it "inscape." Hopkins was also divided as a Catholic, attempting to follow the teachings of both Duns Scotus, the Catholic philosopher who taught that the physical world was holy, and St. Ignatius Loyola (founder of the Jesuit Order and author of its manual, the *Spiritual Exercises*), who taught that the physical world was wicked.

This silence lasted for seven years. Then, prompted by the drowning of five German nuns in a shipwreck off the coast of Wales, and encouraged by a superior of his order, he began an elegy that grew to great length and formidable complexity, embodying spiritual and poetic ideas that had never in his life found expression. The result was "The Wreck of the Deutschland," which, more resembling a Greek ode than a dolorous requiem, was rejected by the Jesuit *Month* magazine. But Hopkins' muse had returned with a new maturity and gusto. Thereafter he continued to write, on his priestly travels (which kept him on the move from Oxford to Wales, Lancashire, Scotland, Liverpool and finally Dublin), collecting his impressions and cultivating his new poetic, using a rhythmic method he called "Sprung" (explained at length in the "Author's Preface," beginning on page vii of this volume).

The first-time reader of the poems will recognize at once that Hopkins achieved a major departure from English poetry of the day (of which his own favorite writer was Christina Rossetti, herself not the most visible poet of the era). This is especially evident when the poems are read aloud, which the poet especially desired they should be. Despite his seeming exoticism, however, Hopkins arrived at his poetic ideas by a distillation of English verse to its organic basics, namely the diction and alliterative phonic values of Anglo-Saxon poetry. In the Old English language, Hopkins discovered a ruggedness and plasticity (qualities he also admired in Ancient Greek) and began to favor the Anglo-Saxon end of English vocabulary (as opposed to the Latinate). He noticed that sounds in alliterative verse did not merely complement each other ornamentally, but actually suggested each other, building on each other as in the growth of crystals. The poet adopted this for his chief creative principle. The result in Hopkins' work is not only a new range of sound in English poetry, but, strange though it may seem, an illustration of the working of *natural* speech. Thus, our reaction to the strange and opulent music of Hopkins' poetry is not only one of amazement, but, really, of recognition.

A word or two should be devoted to two terms with which any reader of Hopkins should be familiar, namely "inscape" and "instress." As briefly mentioned above, "inscape" is the reunification through the senses, of the world about one so that its own essential beauty (or at any rate its essence) is seen. The "instress" is the presence of a primary energy (God) which, in an individual's perception of the inscape, reveals itself.

Fortunately, Hopkins' obscurity was not complete, and it is through his correspondence with the poet and physician Robert Bridges, a close friend at Oxford, later the Poet Laureate of England (succeeding Sir Alfred Austin), that we know Hopkins, and have a surviving body of poems.

The present edition includes all the finished poems from the first edition (1918); their dates of composition range between 1876 and 1889. A new set of explanatory notes (each signaled by an asterisk in the text) appears at the end of the volume.

Contents

Author's Preface

THE POEMS in this book[1] are written some in Running Rhythm, the common rhythm in English use, some in Sprung Rhythm, and some in a mixture of the two. And those in the common rhythm are some counterpointed, some not.

Common English rhythm, called Running Rhythm above, is measured by feet of either two or three syllables and (putting aside the imperfect feet at the beginning and end of lines and also some unusual measures, in which feet seem to be paired together and double or composite feet to arise) never more or less.

Every foot has one principal stress or accent, and this or the syllable it falls on may be called the Stress of the foot and the other part, the one or two unaccented syllables, the Slack. Feet (and the rhythms made out of them) in which the stress comes first are called Falling Feet and Falling Rhythms, feet and rhythm in which the slack comes first are called Rising Feet and Rhythms, and if the stress is between two slacks there will be Rocking Feet and Rhythms. These distinctions are real and true to nature; but for purposes of scanning it is a great convenience to follow the example of music and take the stress always first, as the accent or the chief accent always comes first in a musical bar. If this is done there will be in common English verse only two possible feet — the so-called accentual Trochee and Dactyl, and correspondingly only two possible uniform rhythms, the so-called Trochaic and Dactylic. But they may be mixed and then what the Greeks called a Logaoedic Rhythm arises. These are the facts and according to these the scanning of ordinary regularly-written English verse is very simple indeed and to bring in other principles is here unnecessary.

But because verse written strictly in these feet and by these principles will become same and tame the poets have brought in licences and departures from rule to give variety, and especially when the natural rhythm is rising, as in the common ten-syllable or five-foot verse, rhymed or blank. These irregularities are chiefly Reversed Feet and

---

[1] The notebook in which Robert Bridges kept Hopkins' work; substantially what survives of the poetry and the basis of the 1918 First Edition.

Reversed or Counterpoint Rhythm, which two things are two steps or degrees of licence in the same kind. By a reversed foot I mean the putting the stress where, to judge by the rest of the measure, the slack should be and the slack where the stress, and this is done freely at the beginning of a line and, in the course of a line, after a pause; only scarcely ever in the second foot or place and never in the last, unless when the poet designs some extraordinary effect; for these places are characteristic and sensitive and cannot well be touched. But the reversal of the first foot and of some middle foot after a strong pause is a thing so natural that our poets have generally done it, from Chaucer down, without remark and it commonly passes unnoticed and cannot be said to amount to a formal change of rhythm, but rather is that irregularity which all natural growth and motion shews. If however the reversal is repeated in two feet running, especially so as to include the sensitive second foot, it must be due either to great want of ear or else is a calculated effect, the superinducing or *mounting* of a new rhythm upon the old; and since the new or mounted rhythm is actually heard and at the same time the mind naturally supplies the natural or standard foregoing rhythm, for we do not forget what the rhythm is that by rights we should be hearing, two rhythms are in some manner running at once and we have something answerable to counterpoint in music, which is two or more strains of tune going on together, and this is Counterpoint Rhythm. Of this kind of verse Milton is the great master and the choruses of *Samson Agonistes*[2] are written throughout in it — but with the disadvantage that he does not let the reader clearly know what the ground-rhythm is meant to be and so they have struck most readers as merely irregular. And in fact if you counterpoint throughout, since one only of the counter rhythms is actually heard, the other is really destroyed or cannot come to exist, and what is written is one rhythm only and probably Sprung Rhythm, of which I now speak.

Sprung Rhythm, as used in this book, is measured by feet of from one to four syllables, regularly, and for particular effects any number of weak or slack syllables may be used. It has one stress, which falls on the only

---

[2] For example:

> Or do my eyes misrepresent? Can this be he,
> That heroic, that renowned,
> Irresistible Samson? whom, unarmed,
> No strength of man, or fiercest wild beast, could withstand; . . .

syllable, if there is only one, or, if there are more, then scanning as above, on the first, and so gives rise to four sorts of feet, a monosyllable and the so-called accentual Trochee, Dactyl, and the First Paeon. And there will be four corresponding natural rhythms; but nominally the feet are mixed and any one may follow any other. And hence Sprung Rhythm differs from Running Rhythm in having or being only one nominal rhythm, a mixed or 'logaoedic' one, instead of three, but on the other hand in having twice the flexibility of foot, so that any two stresses may either follow one another running or be divided by one, two, or three slack syllables. But strict Sprung Rhythm cannot be counterpointed. In Sprung Rhythm, as in logaoedic rhythm generally, the feet are assumed to be equally long or strong and their seeming inequality is made up by pause or stressing.

Remark also that it is natural in Sprung Rhythm for the lines to be *rove over*, that is for the scanning of each line immediately to take up that of the one before, so that if the first has one or more syllables at its end the other must have so many the less at its beginning; and in fact the scanning runs on without break from the beginning, say, of a stanza to the end and all the stanza is one long strain, though written in lines asunder.

Two licences are natural to Sprung Rhythm. The one is rests, as in music; but of this an example is scarcely to be found in this book, unless in the *Echos*,[3] second line. The other is *hangers* or *outrides*, that is one, two, or three slack syllables added to a foot and not counting in the nominal scanning. They are so called because they seem to hang below the line or ride forward or backward from it in another dimension than the line itself, according to a principle needless to explain here. These outriding half feet or hangers are marked by a loop underneath them, and plenty of them will be found.

The other marks are easily understood, namely accents, where the reader might be in doubt which syllable should have the stress; slurs, that is loops *over* syllables, to tie them together into the time of one; little loops at the end of a line to shew that the rhyme goes on to the first letter of the next line; what in music are called pauses ⌢, to shew that the syllable should be dwelt on; and twirls ~ , to mark reversed or counterpointed rhythm.[4]

Note on the nature and history of Sprung Rhythm — Sprung Rhythm is the most natural of things. For (1) it is the rhythm of common speech

---

[3] Cf. page 37.

[4] Bridges removed these marks when preparing the poems for publication. The rhythmic features they describe, however, are readily discernible to the ear.

and of written prose, when rhythm is perceived in them. (2) It is the rhythm of all but the most monotonously regular music, so that in the words of choruses and refrains and in songs written closely to music it arises. (3) It is found in nursery rhymes, weather saws, and so on; because, however these may have been once made in running rhythm, the terminations having dropped off by the change of language, the stresses come together and so the rhythm is sprung. (4) It arises in common verse when reversed or counterpointed, for the same reason.

But nevertheless in spite of all this and though Greek and Latin lyric verse, which is well known, and the old English verse seen in *Pierce Ploughman* are in sprung rhythm, it has in fact ceased to be used since the Elizabethan age, Greene being the last writer who can be said to have recognised it. For perhaps there was not, down to our days, a single, even short, poem in English in which sprung rhythm is employed — not for single effects or in fixed places — but as the governing principle of the scansion. I say this because the contrary has been asserted: if it is otherwise the poem should be cited.[5]

Some of the sonnets in this book are in five-foot, some in six-foot or Alexandrine lines.

Nos. 13 and 22 are Curtal-Sonnets, that is they are constructed in proportions resembling those of the sonnet proper, namely 6 + 4 instead of 8 + 6, with however a halfline tailpiece (so that the equation is rather $1\frac{1}{2} + \frac{1}{2} = 2\frac{1}{2} = 10\frac{1}{2}$).

---

[5] The challenge is to Bridges.

1

For a Picture of St. Dorothea*

I bear a basket lined with grass;
I am so light, I am so fair,
That men must wonder as I pass
And at the basket that I bear,
Where in a newly-drawn green litter
Sweet flowers I carry, — sweets for bitter.

Lilies I shew you, lilies none,
None in Caesar's gardens blow, —
And a quince in hand, — not one
Is set upon your boughs below;
Not set, because their buds not spring;
Spring not, 'cause world is wintering.

But these were found in the East and South
Where Winter is the clime forgot. —
The dewdrop on the larkspur's mouth
O should it then be quenchèd not?
In starry water-meads they drew
These drops: which be they? stars or dew?

Had she a quince in hand? Yet gaze:
Rather it is the sizing moon.
Lo, linkèd heavens with milky ways!
That was her larkspur row. — So soon?
Sphered so fast, sweet soul? — We see
Nor fruit, nor flowers, nor Dorothy.

2

Heaven-Haven

A nun takes the veil

I have desired to go
    Where springs not fail,
To fields where flies no sharp and sided hail
    And a few lilies blow.

---

* Asterisks refer to end-notes, beginning on page 51.

1

And I have asked to be
Where no storms come,
Where the green swell is in the havens dumb,
And out of the swing of the sea.

3

The Habit of Perfection

Elected Silence, sing to me
And beat upon my whorlèd ear,
Pipe me to pastures still and be
The music that I care to hear.

Shape nothing, lips; be lovely-dumb:
It is the shut, the curfew sent
From there where all surrenders come
Which only makes you eloquent.

Be shellèd, eyes, with double dark
And find the uncreated light:
This ruck and reel which you remark
Coils, keeps, and teases simple sight.

Palate, the hutch of tasty lust,
Desire not to be rinsed with wine:
The can must be so sweet, the crust
So fresh that come in fasts divine!

Nostrils, your careless breath that spend
Upon the stir and keep of pride,
What relish shall the censers send
Along the sanctuary side!

O feel-of-primrose hands, O feet
That want the yield of plushy sward,
But you shall walk the golden street
And you unhouse and house the Lord.

And, Poverty, be thou the bride
And now the marriage feast begun,
And lily-coloured clothes provide
Your spouse not laboured-at nor spun.*

4

The Wreck of the Deutschland

*To the happy memory of five Franciscan Nuns exiles by the Falk
Laws drowned between midnight and morning of Dec. 7th, 1875*

PART THE FIRST

1

      Thou mastering me
    God! giver of breath and bread;
  World's strand, sway of the sea;
    Lord of living and dead;
Thou hast bound bones and veins in me, fastened me flesh,
And after it almost unmade, what with dread,
    Thy doing: and dost thou touch me afresh?
Over again I feel thy finger and find thee.

2

      I did say yes
    O at lightning and lashed rod;
  Thou heardst me truer than tongue confess
    Thy terror, O Christ, O God;
Thou knowest the walls, altar and hour and night:
The swoon of a heart that the sweep and the hurl of thee trod
    Hard down with a horror of height:
And the midriff astrain with leaning of, laced with fire of stress.

3

> The frown of his face
> Before me, the hurtle of hell
> Behind, where, where was a, where was a place?
> I whirled out wings that spell
> And fled with a fling of the heart to the heart of the Host.
> My heart, but you were dovewinged, I can tell,
> Carrier-witted, I am bold to boast,
> To flash from the flame to the flame then, tower from the grace to
> the grace.

4

> I am soft sift
> In an hourglass — at the wall
> Fast, but mined with a motion, a drift,
> And it crowds and it combs to the fall;
> I steady as a water in a well, to a poise, to a pane,
> But roped with, always, all the way down from the tall
> Fells or flanks of the voel, a vein
> Of the gospel proffer, a pressure, a principle, Christ's gift.

5

> I kiss my hand
> To the stars, lovely-asunder
> Starlight, wafting him out of it; and
> Glow, glory in thunder;
> Kiss my hand to the dappled-with-damson west:
> Since, tho' he is under the world's splendour and wonder,
> His mystery must be instressed, stressed;
> For I greet him the days I meet him, and bless when I understand.

6

> Not out of his bliss
> Springs the stress felt
> Nor first from heaven (and few know this)
> Swings the stroke dealt —
> Stroke and a stress that stars and storms deliver,

That guilt is hushed by, hearts are flushed by and melt—
  But it rides time like riding a river
(And here the faithful waver, the faithless'fable and miss).

7

        It dates from day
      Of his going in Galilee;
    Warm-laid grave of a womb-life grey;
      Manger, maiden's knee;
  The dense and the driven Passion, and frightful sweat;
    Thence the discharge of it, there its swelling to be,
      Though felt before, though in high flood yet—
What none would have known of it, only the heart, being hard at
      bay,

8

        Is out with it! Oh,
      We lash with the best or worst
    Word last!   How a lush-kept plush-capped sloe
      Will, mouthed to flesh-burst,
  Gush!—flush the man, the being with it, sour or sweet,
    Brim, in a flash, full!—Hither then, last or first,
      To hero of Calvary, Christ, 's feet—
Never ask if meaning it, wanting it, warned of it—men go.

9

        Be adored among men,
      God, three-numberèd form;
    Wring thy rebel, dogged in den,
      Man's malice, with wrecking and storm.
  Beyond saying sweet, past telling of tongue,
    Thou art lightning and love, I found it, a winter and warm;
      Father and fondler of heart thou hast wrung:
Hast thy dark descending and most art merciful then.

10

        With an anvil-ding
      And with fire in him forge thy will

Or rather, rather then, stealing as Spring
    Through him, melt him but master him still:
Whether at once, as once at a crash Paul,
Or as Austin, a lingering-out sweet skill,
    Make mercy in all of us, out of us all
Mastery, but be adored, but be adored King.

PART THE SECOND

11

        'Some find me a sword; some
            The flange and the rail; flame,
        Fang, or flood' goes Death on drum,
            And storms bugle his fame.
    But wé dream we are rooted in earth — Dust!
    Flesh falls within sight of us, we, though our flower the same,
        Wave with the meadow, forget that there must
    The sour scythe cringe, and the blear share come.

12

        On Saturday sailed from Bremen,
            American-outward-bound,
        Take settler and seamen, tell men with women,
            Two hundred souls in the round —
    O Father, not under thy feathers nor ever as guessing
    The goal was a shoal, of a fourth the doom to be drowned;
        Yet did the dark side of the bay of thy blessing
    Not vault them, the millions of rounds of thy mercy not reeve even
        them in?

13

        Into the snows she sweeps,
            Hurling the haven behind,
        The Deutschland, on Sunday; and so the sky keeps,
            For the infinite air is unkind,
    And the sea flint-flake, black-backed in the regular blow,

Sitting Eastnortheast, in cursed quarter, the wind;
　　Wiry and white-fiery and whirlwind-swivellèd snow
Spins to the widow-making unchilding unfathering deeps.

14

　　　　She drove in the dark to leeward,
　　　　She struck — not a reef or a rock
　　But the combs of a smother of sand: night drew her
　　　　Dead to the Kentish Knock;*
And she beat the bank down with her bows and the ride of her keel:
　　The breakers rolled on her beam with ruinous shock;
　　　　And canvas and compass, the whorl and the wheel
Idle for ever to waft her or wind her with, these she endured.

15

　　　　Hope had grown grey hairs,
　　　　Hope had mourning on,
　　Trenched with tears, carved with cares,
　　　　Hope was twelve hours gone;
And frightful a nightfall folded rueful a day
　　Nor rescue, only rocket and lightship, shone,
　　　　And lives at last were washing away:
To the shrouds they took, — they shook in the hurling and horrible
　　airs.

16

　　　　One stirred from the rigging to save
　　　　The wild woman-kind below,
　　With a rope's end round the man, handy and brave —
　　　　He was pitched to his death at a blow,
For all his dreadnought breast and braids of thew:
　　They could tell him for hours, dandled the to and fro
　　　　Through the cobbled foam-fleece, what could he do
With the burl of the fountains of air, buck and the flood of the wave?

17

　　　　They fought with God's cold —
　　　　And they could not and fell to the deck
　　(Crushed them) or water (and drowned them) or rolled

With the sea-romp over the wreck.
Night roared, with the heart-break hearing a heart-broke
rabble,
The woman's wailing, the crying of child without check —
Till a lioness arose breasting the babble,
A prophetess towered in the tumult, a virginal tongue told.

18

Ah, touched in your bower of bone
Are you! turned for an exquisite smart,
Have you! make words break from me here all alone,
Do you! — mother of being in me, heart.
O unteachably after evil, but uttering truth,
Why tears! is it? tears; such a melting, a madrigal start!
Never-eldering revel and river of youth,
What can it be, this glee? the good you have there of your
own?

19

Sister, a sister calling
A master, her master and mine! —
And the inboard seas run swirling and hawling;
The rash smart sloggering brine
Blinds her; but she that weather sees one thing, one;
Has one fetch in her: she rears herself to divine
Ears, and the call of the tall nun
To the men in the tops and the tackle rode over the storm's
brawling.

20

She was first of a five and came
Of a coifèd sisterhood.
(O Deutschland, double a desperate name!
O world wide of its good!
But Gertrude, lily, and Luther, are two of a town,*
Christ's lily and beast of the waste wood:
From life's dawn it is drawn down,
Abel is Cain's brother and breasts they have sucked the same.)

21

> Loathed for a love men knew in them,
> Banned by the land of their birth,
> Rhine refused them.   Thames would ruin them;
> Surf, snow, river and earth
> Gnashed: but thou art above, thou Orion of light;
> Thy unchancelling poising palms were weighing the worth,
> Thou martyr-master: in thy sight
> Storm flakes were scroll-leaved flowers, lily showers — sweet
> heaven was astrew in them.

22

> Five! the finding and sake
> And cipher of suffering Christ.
> Mark, the mark is of man's make
> And the word of it Sacrificed.
> But he scores it in scarlet himself on his own bespoken,
> Before-time-taken, dearest prizèd and priced —
> Stigma, signal, cinquefoil token
> For lettering of the lamb's fleece, ruddying of the rose-flake.

23

> Joy fall to thee, father Francis,*
> Drawn to the Life that died;
> With the gnarls of the nails in thee, niche of the lance, his
> Lovescape crucified
> And seal of his seraph-arrival! and these thy daughters
> And five-livèd and leavèd favour and pride,
> Are sisterly sealed in wild waters,
> To bathe in his fall-gold mercies, to breathe in his all-fire glances.

24

> Away in the loveable west,
> On a pastoral forehead of Wales,
> I was under a roof here, I was at rest,
> And they the prey of the gales;
> She to the black-about air, to the breaker, the thickly

Falling flakes, to the throng that catches and quails
  Was calling 'O Christ, Christ, come quickly':
The cross to her she calls Christ to her, christens her wild-worst Best.

25

    The majesty! what did she mean?
      Breathe, arch and original Breath.
  Is it love in her of the being as her lover had been?
      Breathe, body of lovely Death.
  They were else-minded then, altogether, the men
  Woke thee with a *we are perishing* in the weather of Gennesareth.
    Or is it that she cried for the crown then,
The keener to come at the comfort for feeling the combating keen?

26

    For how to the heart's cheering
      The down-dugged ground-hugged grey
  Hovers off, the jay-blue heavens appearing
      Of pied and peeled May!
  Blue-beating and hoary-glow height; or night, still higher,
  With belled fire and the moth-soft Milky Way,
    What by your measure is the heaven of desire,
The treasure never eyesight got, nor was ever guessed what for the
      hearing?

27

    No, but it was not these.
      The jading and jar of the cart,
  Time's tasking, it is fathers that asking for ease
      Of the sodden-with-its-sorrowing heart,
  Not danger, electrical horror; then further it finds
  The appealing of the Passion is tenderer in prayer apart:
    Other, I gather, in measure her mind's
Burden, in wind's burly and beat of endragonèd seas.

28

    But how shall I . . . make me room there:
      Reach me a . . . Fancy, come faster —
  Strike you the sight of it? look at it loom there,

Thing that she . . . there then! the Master,
Ipse, the only one, Christ, King, Head:*
He was to cure the extremity where he had cast her;
    Do, deal, lord it with living and dead;
Let him ride, her pride, in his triumph, despatch and have done
    with his doom there.

29

            Ah! there was a heart right!
            There was single eye!*
    Read the unshapeable shock night
        And knew the who and the why;
    Wording it how but by him that present and past,
    Heaven and earth are word of, worded by? —
        The Simon Peter of a soul! to the blast
Tarpeian-fast, but a blown beacon of light.

30

            Jesu, heart's light,
            Jesu, maid's son,
    What was the feast followed the night
        Thou hadst glory of this nun? —
    Feast of the one woman without stain.
    For so conceivèd, so to conceive thee is done;
        But here was heart-throe, birth of a brain,
Word, that heard and kept thee and uttered thee outright.

31

            Well, she has thee for the pain, for the
            Patience; but pity of the rest of them!
    Heart, go and bleed at a bitterer vein for the
        Comfortless unconfessed of them —
    No not uncomforted: lovely-felicitous Providence
    Finger of a tender of, O of a feathery delicacy, the breast of the
        Maiden could obey so, be a bell to, ring of it, and
Startle the poor sheep back! is the shipwrack then a harvest, does
    tempest carry the grain for thee?

32

>I admire thee, master of the tides,
>   Of the Yore-flood, of the year's fall;
>The recurb and the recovery of the gulf's sides,
>   The girth of it and the wharf of it and the wall;
>Stanching, quenching ocean of a motionable mind;
>Ground of being, and granite of it: past all
>   Grasp God, throned behind
>Death with a sovereignty that heeds but hides, bodes but abides;

33

>With a mercy that outrides
>   The all of water, an ark
>For the listener; for the lingerer with a love glides
>   Lower than death and the dark;
>A vein for the visiting of the past-prayer, pent in prison,
>The-last-breath penitent spirits — the uttermost mark
>   Our passion-plungèd giant risen,
>The Christ of the Father compassionate, fetched in the storm of his
>   strides.

34

>Now burn, new born to the world,
>   Doubled-naturèd name,
>The heaven-flung, heart-fleshed, maiden-furled
>   Miracle-in-Mary-of-flame,
>Mid-numbered He in three of the thunder-throne!
>Not a dooms-day dazzle in his coming nor dark as he came;
>   Kind, but royally reclaiming his own;
>A released shower, let flash to the shire, not a lightning of fire hard-
>   hurled.

35

>Dame, at our door
>   Drowned, and among our shoals,
>Remember us in the roads, the heaven-haven of the Reward:
>   Our King back, oh, upon English souls!
>Let him easter in us, be a dayspring to the dimness of us, be a
>   crimson-cresseted east,

More brightening her, rare-dear Britain, as his reign rolls,
    Pride, rose, prince, hero of us, high-priest,
Our hearts' charity's hearth's fire, our thoughts' chivalry's throng's
    Lord.

5

Penmaen Pool

For the Visitors' Book at the Inn

Who long for rest, who look for pleasure
Away from counter, court, or school
O where live well your lease of leisure
But here at, here at Penmaen Pool?

You'll dare the Alp? you'll dart the skiff? —
Each sport has here its tackle and tool:
Come, plant the staff by Cadair cliff;
Come, swing the sculls on Penmaen Pool.

What's yonder? — Grizzled Dyphwys dim:
The triple-hummocked Giant's stool,
Hoar messmate, hobs and nobs with him
To halve the bowl of Penmaen Pool.

And all the landscape under survey,
At tranquil turns, by nature's rule,
Rides repeated topsyturvy
In frank, in fairy Penmaen Pool.

And Charles's Wain, the wondrous seven,
And sheep-flock clouds like worlds of wool,
For all they shine so, high in heaven,
Shew brighter shaken in Penmaen Pool.

The Mawddach, how she trips ! though throttled
If floodtide teeming thrills her full,
And mazy sands all water-wattled
Waylay her at ebb, past Penmaen Pool.

But what's to see in stormy weather,
When grey showers gather and gusts are cool? —
Why, raindrop-roundels looped together
That lace the face of Penmaen Pool.

Then even in weariest wintry hour
Of New Year's month or surly Yule
Furred snows, charged tuft above tuft, tower
From darksome darksome Penmaen Pool.

And ever, if bound here hardest home,
You've parlour-pastime left and (who'll
Not honour it?) ale like goldy foam
That frocks an oar in Penmaen Pool.

Then come who pine for peace or pleasure
Away from counter, court, or school,
Spend here your measure of time and treasure
And taste the treats of Penmaen Pool.

6

The Silver Jubilee:

*To James First Bishop of Shrewsbury on the 25th Year of his
Episcopate July 28, 1876*

1

Though no high-hung bells or din
Of braggart bugles cry it in —
    What is sound? Nature's round
Makes the Silver Jubilee.

2

Five and twenty years have run
Since sacred fountains to the sun
    Sprang, that but now were shut,
Showering Silver Jubilee.

3

Feasts, when we shall fall asleep,
Shrewsbury may see others keep;
   None but you this her true,
This her Silver Jubilee.

4

Not today we need lament
Your wealth of life is some way spent:
   Toil has shed round your head
Silver but for Jubilee.

5

Then for her whose velvet vales
Should have pealed with welcome, Wales,
   Let the chime of a rhyme
Utter Silver Jubilee.

7

God's Grandeur

The world is charged with the grandeur of God.
   It will flame out, like shining from shook foil;
   It gathers to a greatness, like the ooze of oil
Crushed. Why do men then now not reck his rod?
Generations have trod, have trod, have trod;
   And all is seared with trade; bleared, smeared with toil;
   And wears man's smudge and shares man's smell: the soil
Is bare now, nor can foot feel, being shod.

And for all this, nature is never spent;
   There lives the dearest freshness deep down things;
And though the last lights off the black West went
   Oh, morning, at the brown brink eastward, springs —
Because the Holy Ghost over the bent
   World broods with warm breast and with ah! bright wings.

8

The Starlight Night

Look at the stars! look, look up at the skies!
    O look at all the fire-folk sitting in the air!
    The bright boroughs, the circle-citadels there!
Down in dim woods the diamond delves! the elves'-eyes!
The grey lawns cold where gold, where quickgold lies!
    Wind-beat whitebeam! airy abeles set on a flare!
    Flake-doves sent floating forth at a farmyard scare! —
Ah well! it is all a purchase, all is a prize.

Buy then! bid then! — What? — Prayer, patience, alms, vows.
Look, look: a May-mess, like on orchard boughs!
    Look! March-bloom, like on mealed-with-yellow sallows!
These are indeed the barn; withindoors house
The shocks. This piece-bright paling shuts the spouse
    Christ home, Christ and his mother and all his hallows.

9

Spring

Nothing is so beautiful as spring —
    When weeds, in wheels, shoot long and lovely and lush;
    Thrush's eggs look little low heavens, and thrush
Through the echoing timber does so rinse and wring
The ear, it strikes like lightnings to hear him sing;
    The glassy peartree leaves and blooms, they brush
    The descending blue; that blue is all in a rush
With richness; the racing lambs too have fair their fling.

What is all this juice and all this joy?
    A strain of the earth's sweet being in the beginning
In Eden garden. — Have, get, before it cloy,
    Before it cloud, Christ, lord, and sour with sinning,
Innocent mind and Mayday in girl and boy,
    Most, O maid's child, thy choice and worthy the winning.

10

The Lantern out of Doors

Sometimes a lantern moves along the night,
   That interests our eyes. And who goes there?
   I think; where from and bound, I wonder, where,
With, all down darkness wide, his wading light?

Men go by me whom either beauty bright
   In mould or mind or what not else makes rare:
   They rain against our much-thick and marsh air
Rich beams, till death or distance buys them quite.

Death or distance soon consumes them: wind
   What most I may eye after, be in at the end
I cannot, and out of sight is out of mind.

Christ minds; Christ's interest, what to avow or amend
   There, éyes them, heart wánts, care haúnts, foot fóllows kínd,
Their ránsom, théir rescue, ánd first, fást, last friénd.

11

The Sea and the Skylark

On ear and ear two noises too old to end
   Trench — right, the tide that ramps against the shore;
   With a flood or a fall, low lull-off or all roar,
Frequenting there while moon shall wear and wend.

Left hand, off land, I hear the lark ascend,
   His rash-fresh re-winded new-skeinèd score
   In crisps of curl off wild winch whirl, and pour
And pelt music, till none's to spill nor spend.

How these two shame this shallow and frail town!
   How ring right out our sordid turbid time,
Being pure!   We, life's pride and cared-for crown,

Have lost that cheer and charm of earth's past prime:
Our make and making break, are breaking, down
To man's last dust, drain fast towards man's first slime.

12

The Windhover:

To Christ our Lord

I caught this morning morning's minion, king-
 dom of daylight's dauphin, dapple-dawn-drawn Falcon, in his
  riding
Of the rolling level underneath him steady air, and striding
High there, how he rung upon the rein of a wimpling wing
In his ecstasy! then off, off forth on swing,
 As a skate's heel sweeps smooth on a bow-bend: the hurl and
  gliding
Rebuffed the big wind.   My heart in hiding
Stirred for a bird, — the achieve of, the mastery of the thing!

Brute beauty and valour and act, oh, air, pride, plume, here
 Buckle! AND the fire that breaks from thee then, a billion
Times told lovelier, more dangerous, O my chevalier!

No wonder of it: shéer plód makes plough down sillion
Shine, and blue-bleak embers, ah my dear,
 Fall, gall themselves, and gash gold-vermilion.

13

Pied Beauty

Glory be to God for dappled things —
 For skies of couple-colour as a brinded cow;
  For rose-moles all in stipple upon trout that swim;
Fresh-firecoal chestnut-falls; finches' wings;
 Landscape plotted and pieced — fold, fallow, and plough;
  And áll trádes, their gear and tackle and trim.

All things counter, original, sparc, strange;
   Whatever is fickle, freckled (who knows how?)
    With swift, slow; sweet, sour; adazzle, dim;
He fathers-forth whose beauty is past change:
        Praise him.

14

Hurrahing in Harvest

Summer ends now; now, barbarous in beauty, the stooks arisc
   Around; up above, what wind-walks! what lovely behaviour
   Of silk-sack clouds! has wilder, wilful-wavier
Meal-drift moulded ever and melted across skies?

I walk, I lift up, I lift up heart, eyes,
   Down all that glory in the heavens to glean our Saviour;
   And, éyes, heárt, what looks, what lips yet gave you a
Rapturous love's greeting of realer, of rounder replies?

And the azurous hung hills are his world-wielding shoulder
   Majestic — as a stallion stalwart, very-violet-sweet! —
These things, these things were here and but the beholder
   Wanting; which two when they once meet,
The heart rears wings bold and bolder
   And hurls for him, O half hurls earth for him off under his feet.

15

The Caged Skylark

As a dare-gale skylark scanted in a dull cage
   Man's mounting spirit in his bone-house, mean house, dwells —
   That bird beyond the remembering his free fells;
This in drudgery, day-labouring-out life's age.

Though aloft on turf or perch or poor low stage,
   Both sing sometímes the sweetest, sweetest spells,
   Yet both droop deadly sómetimes in their cells
Or wring their barriers in bursts of fear or rage.

Not that the sweet-fowl, song-fowl, needs no rest —
Why, hear him, hear him babble and drop down to his nest,
    But his own nest, wild nest, no prison.

Man's spirit will be flesh-bound when found at best,
But uncumbered: meadow-down is not distressed
    For a rainbow footing it nor he for his bónes rísen.

16

In the Valley of the Elwy

I remember a house where all were good
    To me, God knows, deserving no such thing:
    Comforting smell breathed at very entering,
Fetched fresh, as I suppose, off some sweet wood.
That cordial air made those kind people a hood
    All over, as a bevy of eggs the mothering wing
    Will, or mild nights the new morsels of spring:
Why, it seemed of course; seemed of right it should.

Lovely the woods, waters, meadows, combes, vales,
All the air things wear that build this world of Wales;
    Only the inmate does not correspond:
God, lover of souls, swaying considerate scales,
Complete thy creature dear O where it fails,
    Being mighty a master, being a father and fond.

17

The Loss of the Eurydice

Foundered March 24, 1878

The Eurydice — it concerned thee, O Lord:
Three hundred souls, O alas! on board,
    Some asleep unawakened, all un-
warned, eleven fathoms fallen

Where she foundered! One stroke
Felled and furled them, the hearts of oak!
    And flockbells off the aerial
Downs' forefalls beat to the burial.

For did she pride her, freighted fully, on
Bounden bales or a hoard of bullion? —
    Precious passing measure,
Lads·and men her lade and treasure.

She had come from a cruise, training seamen —
Men, boldboys soon to be men:
    Must it, worst weather,
Blast bole and bloom together?

No Atlantic squall overwrought her
Or rearing billow of the Biscay water:
    Home was hard at hand
And the blow bore from land.

And you were a liar, O blue March day.
Bright sun lanced fire in the heavenly bay;
    But what black Boreas wrecked her? he
Came equipped, deadly-electric,

A beetling baldbright cloud thorough England
Riding: there did storms not mingle? and
    Hailropes hustle and grind their
Heavengravel? wolfsnow, worlds of it, wind there?

Now Carisbrook keep goes under in gloom;
Now it overvaults Appledurcombe;
    Now near by Ventnor town
It hurls, hurls off Boniface Down.

Too proud, too proud, what a press she bore!
Royal, and all her royals wore.
    Sharp with her, shorten sail!
Too late; lost; gone with the gale.

This was that fell capsize,
As half she had righted and hoped to rise

Death teeming in by her portholes
Raced down decks, round messes of mortals.

Then a lurch forward, frigate and men;
'All hands for themselves' the cry ran then;
    But she who had housed them thither
Was around them, bound them or wound them with her.

Marcus Hare, high her captain,
Kept to her — care-drowned and wrapped in
    Cheer's death, would follow
His charge through the champ-white water-in-a-wallow,

All under Channel to bury in a beach her
Cheeks: Right, rude of feature,
    He thought he heard say
'Her commander! and thou too, and thou this way.'

It is even seen, time's something server,
In mankind's medley a duty-swerver,
    At downright 'No or yes?'
Doffs all, drives full for righteousness.

Sydney Fletcher, Bristol-bred,
(Low lie his mates now on watery bed)
    Takes to the seas and snows
As sheer down the ship goes.

Now her afterdraught gullies him too down;
Now he wrings for breath with the deathgush brown;
    Till a lifebelt and God's will
Lend him a lift from the sea-swill.

Now he shoots short up to the round air;
Now he gasps, now he gazes everywhere;
    But his eye no cliff, no coast or
Mark makes in the rivelling snowstorm.

Him, after an hour of wintry waves,
A schooner sights, with another, and saves,

And he boards her in Oh! such joy
He has lost count what came next, poor boy. —

They say who saw one sea-corpse cold
He was all of lovely manly mould,
    Every inch a tar,
Of the best we boast our sailors are.

Look, foot to forelock, how all things suit! he
Is strung by duty, is strained to beauty,
    And brown-as-dawning-skinned
With brine and shine and whirling wind.

O his nimble finger, his gnarled grip!
Leagues, leagues of seamanship
    Slumber in these forsaken
Bones, this sinew, and will not waken.

He was but one like thousands more,
Day and night I deplore
    My people and born own nation,
Fast foundering own generation.

I might let bygones be — our curse
Of ruinous shrine no hand or, worse,
    Robbery's hand is busy to
Dress, hoar-hallowèd shrines unvisited;

Only the breathing temple and fleet
Life, this wildworth blown so sweet,
    These daredeaths, ay this crew, in
Unchrist, all rolled in ruin —

Deeply surely I need to deplore it,
Wondering why my master bore it,
    The riving off that race
So at home, time was, to his truth and grace

That a starlight-wender of ours would say
The marvellous Milk was Walsingham Way

And one — but let be, let be:
More, more than was will yet be. —

O well wept, mother have lost son;
Wept, wife; wept, sweetheart would be one:
    Though grief yield them no good
Yet shed what tears sad truelove should.

But to Christ lord of thunder
Crouch; lay knee by earth low under:
    'Holiest, loveliest, bravest,
Save my hero, O Hero savest.

And the prayer thou hearst me making
Have, at the awful overtaking,
    Heard; have heard and granted
Grace that day grace was wanted.'

Not that hell knows redeeming,
But for souls sunk in seeming
    Fresh, till doomfire burn all,
Prayer shall fetch pity eternal.

18

The May Magnificat

May is Mary's month, and I
Muse at that and wonder why:
    Her feasts follow reason,
    Dated due to season —

Candlemas, Lady Day;
But the Lady Month, May,
    Why fasten that upon her,
    With a feasting in her honour?

Is it only its being brighter
Than the most are must delight her?

Is it opportunest
And flowers finds soonest?

Ask of her, the mighty mother:
Her reply puts this other
    Question: What is Spring? —
    Growth in every thing—

Flesh and fleece, fur and feather,
Grass and greenworld all together;
    Star-eyed strawberry-breasted
    Throstle above her nested

Cluster of bugle blue eggs thin
Forms and warms the life within;
    And bird and blossom swell
    In sod or sheath or shell.

All things rising, all things sizing
Mary sees, sympathising
    With that world of good,
    Nature's motherhood.

Their magnifying of each its kind
With delight calls to mind
    How she did in her stored
    Magnify the Lord.

Well but there was more than this:
Spring's universal bliss
    Much, had much to say
    To offering Mary May.

When drop-of-blood-and-foam-dapple
Bloom lights the orchard-apple
    And thicket and thorp are merry
    With silver-surfèd cherry

And azuring-over greybell makes
Wood banks and brakes wash wet like lakes

And magic cuckoocall
Caps, clears, and clinches all —

This ecstasy all through mothering earth
Tells Mary her mirth till Christ's birth
    To remember and exultation
    In God who was her salvation.

19

Binsey Poplars

felled 1879

My aspens dear, whose airy cages quelled,
Quelled or quenched in leaves the leaping sun,
All felled, felled, are all felled;
    Of a fresh and following folded rank
            Not spared, not one
            That dandled a sandalled
        Shadow that swam or sank
On meadow and river and wind-wandering weed-winding bank.

O if we but knew what we do
        When we delve or hew —
    Hack and rack the growing green!
        Since country is so tender
    To touch, her being só slender,
    That, like this sleek and seeing ball
    But a prick will make no eye at all,
    Where we, even where we mean
            To mend her we end her,
        When we hew or delve:
After-comers cannot guess the beauty been.
    Ten or twelve, only ten or twelve
        Strokes of havoc únselve
            The sweet especial scene,
        Rural scene, a rural scene,
        Sweet especial rural scene.

20

Duns Scotus's Oxford*

Towery city and branchy between towers;
Cuckoo-echoing, bell-swarmèd, lark-charmèd, rook-racked, river-
    rounded;
The dapple-eared lily below thee; that country and town did
Once encounter in, here coped and poisèd powers;

Thou hast a base and brickish skirt there, sours
That neighbour-nature thy grey beauty is grounded
Best in; graceless growth, thou hast confounded
Rural rural keeping — folk, flocks, and flowers.

Yet ah! this air I gather and I release
He lived on; these weeds and waters, these walls are what
He haunted who of all men most sways my spirits to peace;

Of realty the rarest-veinèd unraveller; a not
Rivalled insight, be rival Italy or Greece;
Who fired France for Mary without spot.

21

Henry Purcell*

*The poet wishes well to the divine genius of Purcell and praises him
that, whereas other musicians have given utterance to the moods of
man's mind, he has, beyond that, uttered in notes the very make and
species of man as created both in him and in all men generally.*

Have fair fallen, O fair, fair have fallen, so dear
To me, so arch-especial a spirit as heaves in Henry Purcell,
An age is now since passed, since parted; with the reversal
Of the outward sentence low lays him, listed to a heresy, here.

Not mood in him nor meaning, proud fire or sacred fear,
Or love or pity or all that sweet notes not his might nursle:

It is the forgèd feature finds me; it is the rehearsal
Of own, of abrupt self there so thrusts on, so throngs the ear.

Let him oh! with his air of angels then lift me, lay me! only I'll
Have an eye to the sakes of him, quaint moonmarks, to his pelted
    plumage under
Wings: so some great stormfowl, whenever he has walked his while

The thunder-purple seabeach plumèd purple-of-thunder,
If a wuthering of his palmy snow-pinions scatter a colossal smile
Off him, but meaning motion fans fresh our wits with wonder.

22

Peace

When will you ever, Peace, wild wooddove, shy wings shut,
Your round me roaming end, and under be my boughs?
When, when, Peace, will you, Peace? I'll not play hypocrite
To own my heart: I yield you do come sometimes; but
That piecemeal peace is poor peace. What pure peace allows
Alarms of wars, the daunting wars, the death of it?

O surely, reaving Peace, my Lord should leave in lieu
Some good! And so he does leave Patience exquisite,
That plumes to Peace thereafter. And when Peace here does house
He comes with work to do, he does not come to coo,
    He comes to brood and sit.

23

The Bugler's First Communion

A bugler boy from barrack (it is over the hill
There) — boy bugler, born, he tells me, of Irish
    Mother to an English sire (he
Shares their best gifts surely, fall how things will),

This very very day came down to us after a boon he on
My late being there begged of me, overflowing

Boon in my bestowing,
Came, I say, this day to it — to a First Communion.

Here he knelt then ín regimental red.
Forth Christ from cupboard fetched, how fain I of feet
     To his youngster take his treat!
Low-latched in leaf-light housel his too huge godhead.

There! and your sweetest sendings, ah divine,
By it, heavens, befall him! as a heart Christ's darling, dauntless;
     Tongue true, vaunt- and tauntless;
Breathing bloom of a chastity in mansex fine.

Frowning and forefending angel-warder
Squander the hell-rook ranks sally to molest him;
     March, kind comrade, abreast him;
Dress his days to a dexterous and starlight order.

How it dóes my heart good, visiting at that bleak hill,
When limber liquid youth, that to all I teach
     Yields tender as a pushed peach,
Hies headstrong to its wellbeing of a self-wise self-will!

Then though I should tread tufts of consolation
Dáys áfter, só I in a sort deserve to
     And do serve God to serve to
Just such slips of soldiery Christ's royal ration.

Nothing élse is like it, no, not all so strains
Us: fresh youth fretted in a bloomfall all portending
     That sweet's sweeter ending;
Realm both Christ is heir to and thére réigns.

O now well work that sealing sacred ointment!
O for now charms, arms, what bans off bad
     And locks love ever in a lad!
Let mé though see no more of him, and not disappointment

Those sweet hopes quell whose least me quickenings lift,
In scarlet or somewhere of some day seeing
     That brow and bead of being,
An our day's God's own Galahad. Though this child's drift

Seems by a divíne doom chánnelled, nor do I cry
Disaster there; but may he not rankle and roam
    In backwheels though bound home? —
That left to the Lord of the Eucharist, I here lie by;

Recorded only, I have put my lips on pleas
Would brandle adamantine heaven with ride and jar, did
    Prayer go disregarded:
Forward-like, but however, and like favourable heaven heard these.

24

Morning Midday and Evening Sacrifice

The dappled die-away
Cheek and wimpled lip,
The gold-wisp, the airy-grey
Eye, all in fellowship —
This, all this beauty blooming,
This, all this freshness fuming,
Give God while worth consuming.

Both thought and thew now bolder
And told by Nature: Tower;
Head, heart, hand, heel, and shoulder
That beat and breathe in power —
This pride of prime's enjoyment
Take as for tool, not toy meant
And hold at Christ's employment.

The vault and scope and schooling
And mastery in the mind,
In silk-ash kept from cooling,
And ripest under rind —
What life half lifts the latch of,
What hell stalks towards the snatch of,
Your offering, with despatch, of!

25
Andromeda

Now Time's Andromeda on this rock rude,
With not her either beauty's equal or
Her injury's, looks off by both horns of shore,
Her flower, her piece of being, doomed dragon's food.
    Time past she has been attempted and pursued
By many blows and banes; but now hears roar
A wilder beast from West than all were, more
Rife in her wrongs, more lawless, and more lewd.

    Her Perseus linger and leave her tó her extremes? —
Pillowy air he treads a time and hangs
His thoughts on her, forsaken that she seems,
    All while her patience, morselled into pangs,
Mounts; then to alight disarming, no one dreams,
With Gorgon's gear and barebill, thongs and fangs.

26
The Candle Indoors

Some candle clear burns somewhere I come by.
I muse at how its being puts blissful back
With yellowy moisture mild night's blear-all black,
Or to-fro tender trambeams truckle at the eye.
By that window what task what fingers ply,
I plod wondering, a-wanting, just for lack
Of answer the eagerer a-wanting Jessy or Jack
There/ God to aggrándise, God to glorify. — *

Come you indoors, come home; your fading fire
Mend first and vital candle in close heart's vault:
You there are master, do your own desire;
What hinders? Are you beam-blind, yet to a fault
In a neighbour deft-handed? are you that liar
And, cast by conscience out, spendsavour salt?

27

The Handsome Heart:

at a Gracious Answer

'But tell me, child, your choice; what shall I buy
You?' — 'Father, what you buy me I like best.'
With the sweetest air that said, still plied and pressed,
He swung to his first poised purport of reply.

What the heart is! which, like carriers let fly —
Doff darkness, homing nature knows the rest —
To its own fine function, wild and self-instressed,
Falls light as ten years long taught how to and why.

Mannerly-hearted! more than handsome face —
Beauty's bearing or muse of mounting vein,
All, in this case, bathed in high hallowing grace . . .

Of heaven what boon to buy you, boy, or gain
Not granted! — Only . . . O on that path you pace
Run all your race, O brace sterner that strain!

28

At the Wedding March

God with honour hang your head,
Groom, and grace you, bride, your bed
With lissome scions, sweet scions,
Out of hallowed bodies bred.

Each be other's comfort kind:
Déep, déeper than divined,
Divine charity, dear charity,
Fast you ever, fast bind.

Then let the march tread our ears:
I to him turn with tears
Who to wedlock, his wonder wedlock,
Déals tríumph and immortal years.

29

Felix Randal

Felix Randal the farrier, O he is dead then? my duty all ended,
Who have watched his mould of man, big-boned and hardy-
    handsome
Pining, pining, till time when reason rambled in it and some
Fatal four disorders, fleshed there, all contended?

Sickness broke him. Impatient he cursed at first, but mended
Being anointed and all; though a heavenlier heart began some
Months earlier, since I had our sweet reprieve and ransom
Tendered to him. Ah well, God rest him all road ever he offended!

This seeing the sick endears them to us, us too it endears.
My tongue had taught thee comfort, touch had quenched thy tears,
Thy tears that touched my heart, child, Felix, poor Felix Randal;

How far from then forethought of, all thy more boisterous years,
When thou at the random grim forge, powerful amidst peers,
Didst fettle for the great grey drayhorse his bright and battering
    sandal!

30

Brothers

How lovely the elder brother's
Life all laced in the other's,
Lóve-laced! — what once I well
Witnessed; so fortune fell.
When Shrovetide, two years gone,
Our boys' plays brought on
Part was picked for John,
Young Jóhn: then fear, then joy
Ran revel in the elder boy.
Their night was come now; all
Our company thronged the hall;
Henry, by the wall,
Beckoned me beside him:

I came where called, and eyed him
By meanwhiles; making mý play
Turn most on tender byplay.
For, wrung all on love's rack,
My lad, and lost in Jack,
Smiled, blushed, and bit his lip;
Or drove, with a diver's dip,
Clutched hands down through clasped knees —
Truth's tokens tricks like these,
Old telltales, with what stress
He hung on the imp's success.
Now the other was bráss-bóld:
Hé had no work to hold
His heart up at the strain;
Nay, roguish ran the vein.
Two tedious acts were past;
Jack's call and cue at last;
When Henry, heart-forsook,
Dropped eyes and dared not look.
Eh, how áll rúng!
Young dog, he did give tongue!
But Harry — in his hands he has flung
His tear-tricked cheeks of flame
For fond love and for shame.
    Ah Nature, framed in fault,
There's comfort then, there's salt;
Nature, bad, base, and blind,
Dearly thou canst be kind;
There dearly thén, deárly,
I'll cry thou canst be kind.

31

Spring and Fall:

to a young child

Márgarét, are you gríeving
Over Goldengrove unleaving?
Leáves, líke the things of man, you

With your fresh thoughts care for, can you?
Áh! ás the heart grows older
It will come to such sights colder
By and by, nor spare a sigh
Though worlds of wanwood leafmeal lie;
And yet you wíll weep and know why.
Now no matter, child, the name:
Sórrow's spríngs áre the same.
Nor mouth had, no nor mind, expressed
What heart heard of, ghost guessed:
It ís the blight man was born for,
It is Margaret you mourn for.

32

Spelt from Sibyl's Leaves*

Earnest, earthless, equal, attuneable, | vaulty, voluminous, . . stu-
   pendous
Evening strains to be tíme's vást, | womb-of-all, home-of-all, hearse-
   of-all night.
Her fond yellow hornlight wound to the west, | her wild hollow
   hoarlight hung to the height
Waste; her earliest stars, earl-stars, | stárs principal, overbend us,
Fíre-féaturing heaven. For earth | her being has unbound, her
   dapple is at an end, as-
tray or aswarm, all throughther, in throngs; | self ín self steepèd and
   páshed — qúite
Disremembering, dísmémbering | áll now. Heart, you round me
   right
With: Óur évening is over us; óur night | whélms, whélms, ánd will
   end us.
Only the beak-leaved boughs dragonish | damask the tool-smooth
   bleak light; black,
Ever so black on it. Óur tale, O óur oracle! | Lét life, wáned, ah lét
   life wind
Off hér once skéined stained véined varíety | upon, áll on twó
   spools; párt, pen, páck
Now her áll in twó flocks, twó folds — black, white; | right, wrong;
   reckon but, reck but, mind

But thése two; wáre of a wórld where bút these | twó tell, each off
    the óther; of a rack
Where, selfwrung, selfstrung, sheathe- and shelterless, | thóughts
    agaínst thoughts ín groans grínd.

33

Inversnaid

This darksome burn, horseback brown,
His rollrock highroad roaring down,
In coop and in comb the fleece of his foam
Flutes and low to the lake falls home.

A windpuff-bonnet of fáwn-fróth
Turns and twindles over the broth
Of a pool so pitchblack, féll-frówning,
It rounds and rounds Despair to drowning.

Degged with dew, dappled with dew
Are the groins of the braes that the brook treads through,
Wiry heathpacks, flitches of fern,
And the beadbonny ash that sits over the burn.

What would the world be, once bereft
Of wet and of wildness? Let them be left,
O let them be left, wildness and wet;
Long live the weeds and the wilderness yet.

34

As kingfishers catch fire, dragonflies dráw fláme;
As tumbled over rim in roundy wells
Stones ring; like each tucked string tells, each hung bell's
Bow swung finds tongue to fling out broad its name;
Each mortal thing does one thing and the same:
Deals out that being indoors each one dwells;
Selves — goes itself; *myself* it speaks and spells,
Crying *Whát I do is me: for that I came.*

Í say móre: the just man justices;
Kéeps gráce: thát keeps all his goings graces;
Acts in God's eye what in God's eye he is—
Chríst—for Christ plays in ten thousand places,
Lovely in limbs, and lovely in eyes not his
To the Father through the features of men's faces.

35

Ribblesdale

Earth, sweet Earth, sweet landscape, with leavès throng
And louchèd low grass, heaven that dost appeal
To, with no tongue to plead, no heart to feel;
That canst but only be, but dost that long—

Thou canst but be, but that thou well dost; strong
Thy plea with him who dealt, nay docs now deal,
Thy lovely dale down thus and thus bids reel
Thy river, and o'er gives all to rack or wrong.

And what is Earth's eye, tongue, or heart else, where
Else, but in dear and dogged man?—Ah, the heir
To his own selfbent so bound, so tied to his turn,
To thriftless reave both our rich round world bare
And none reck of world after, this bids wear
Earth brows of such care, care and dear concern.

36

The Leaden Echo and the Golden Echo

(*Maidens' song from St. Winefred's Well*)*

THE LEADEN ECHO

How to kéep—is there ány any, is there none such, nowhere
        known some, bow or brooch or braid or brace, láce, latch or
        catch or key to keep

Back beauty, keep it, beauty, beauty, beauty, . . . from vanishing
　　away?
Ó is there no frowning of these wrinkles, rankèd wrinkles deep,
Dówn? no waving off of these most mournful messengers, still
　　messengers, sad and stealing messengers of grey?
No there's none, there's none, O no there's none,
Nor can you long be, what you now are, called fair,
Do what you may do, what, do what you may,
And wisdom is early to despair:
Be beginning; since, no, nothing can be done
To keep at bay
Age and age's evils, hoar hair,
Ruck and wrinkle, drooping, dying, death's worst, winding sheets,
　　tombs and worms and tumbling to decay;
So be beginning, be beginning to despair.
O there's none; no no no there's none:
Be beginning to despair, to despair,
Despair, despair, despair, despair.

THE GOLDEN ECHO

　　　　　Spare!
There ís one, yes I have one (Hush there!);
Only not within seeing of the sun,
Not within the singeing of the strong sun,
Tall sun's tingeing, or treacherous the tainting of the earth's air,
Somewhere elsewhere there is ah well where! one,
Óne. Yes I can tell such a key, I do know such a place,
Where whatever's prized and passes of us, everything that's fresh
　　and fast flying of us, seems to us sweet of us and swiftly away
　　with, done away with, undone,
Undone, done with, soon done with, and yet dearly and danger-
　　ously sweet
Of us, the wimpled-water-dimpled, not-by-morning-matchèd face,
The flower of beauty, fleece of beauty, too too apt to, ah! to fleet,
Never fleets móre, fastened with the tenderest truth
To its own best being and its loveliness of youth: it is an everlasting-
　　ness of, O it is an all youth!
Come then, your ways and airs and looks, locks, maiden gear,
　　gallantry and gaiety and grace,

Winning ways, airs innocent, maiden manners, sweet looks, loose
    locks, long locks, lovelocks, gaygear, going gallant, girl-
    grace —
Resign them, sign them, seal them, send them, motion them with
    breath,
And with sighs soaring, soaring síghs deliver
Them; beauty-in-the-ghost, deliver it, early now, long before death
Give beauty back, beauty, beauty, beauty, back to God, beauty's self
    and beauty's giver.
See; not a hair is, not an eyelash, not the least lash lost; every hair
Is, hair of the head, numbered.
Nay, what we had lighthanded left in surly the mere mould
Will have waked and have waxed and have walked with the wind
    what while we slept,
This side, that side hurling a heavyheaded hundredfold
What while we, while we slumbered.
O then, weary then whý should we tread? O why are we so haggard
    at the heart, so care-coiled, care-killed, so fagged, so fashed, so
    cogged, so cumbered,
When the thing we freely fórfeit is kept with fonder a care,
Fonder a care kept than we could have kept it, kept
Far with fonder a care (and we, we should have lost it) finer, fonder
A care kept. — Where kept? Do but tell us where kept, where. —
Yonder. — What high as that! We follow, now we follow. —
    Yonder, yes yonder, yonder,
Yonder.

37

The Blessed Virgin compared to the Air we Breathe

Wild air, world-mothering air,
Nestling me everywhere,
That each eyelash or hair
Girdles; goes home betwixt
The fleeciest, frailest-fixed
Snowflake; that's fairly mixed
With, riddles, and is rife
In every least thing's life;
This needful, never spent,

And nursing element;
My more than meat and drink,
My meal at every wink;
This air, which, by life's law,
My lung must draw and draw
Now but to breathe its praise,
Minds me in many ways
Of her who not only
Gave God's infinity
Dwindled to infancy
Welcome in womb and breast,
Birth, milk, and all the rest
But mothers each new grace
That does now reach our race —
Mary Immaculate,
Merely a woman, yet
Whose presence, power is
Great as no goddess's
Was deemèd, dreamèd; who
This one work has to do —
Let all God's glory through,
God's glory which would go
Through her and from her flow
Off, and no way but so.

I say that we are wound
With mercy round and round
As if with air: the same
Is Mary, more by name.
She, wild web, wondrous robe,
Mantles the guilty globe,
Since God has let dispense
Her prayers his providence:
Nay, more than almoner,
The sweet alms' self is her
And men are meant to share
Her life as life does air.
If I have understood,
She holds high motherhood
Towards all our ghostly good
And plays in grace her part

About man's beating heart,
Laying, like air's fine flood,
The deathdance in his blood;
Yet no part but what will
Be Christ our Saviour still.
Of her flesh he took flesh:
He does take fresh and fresh,
Though much the mystery how,
Not flesh but spirit now
And makes, O marvellous!
New Nazareths in us,
Where she shall yet conceive
Him, morning, noon, and eve;
New Bethlems, and he born
There, evening, noon, and morn —
Bethlem or Nazareth,
Men here may draw like breath
More Christ and baffle death;
Who, born so, comes to be
New self and nobler me
In each one and each one
More makes, when all is done,
Both God's and Mary's Son.
    Again, look overhead
How air is azurèd;
O how! nay do but stand
Where you can lift your hand
Skywards: rich, rich it laps
Round the four fingergaps.
Yet such a sapphire-shot,
Charged, steepèd sky will not
Stain light.   Yea, mark you this:
It does no prejudice.
The glass-blue days are those
When every colour glows,
Each shape and shadow shows.
Blue be it: this blue heaven
The seven or seven times seven
Hued sunbeam will transmit
Perfect, not alter it.
Or if there does some soft,

On things aloof, aloft,
Bloom breathe, that one breath more
Earth is the fairer for.
Whereas did air not make
This bath of blue and slake
His fire, the sun would shake,
A blear and blinding ball
With blackness bound, and all
The thick stars round him roll
Flashing like flecks of coal,
Quartz-fret, or sparks of salt,
In grimy vasty vault.
    So God was god of old:
A mother came to mould
Those limbs like ours which are
What must make our daystar
Much dearer to mankind;
Whose glory bare would blind
Or less would win man's mind.
Through her we may see him
Made sweeter, not made dim,
And her hand leaves his light
Sifted to suit our sight.
    Be thou then, O thou dear
Mother, my atmosphere;
My happier world, wherein
To wend and meet no sin;
Above me, round me lie
Fronting my froward eye
With sweet and scarless sky;
Stir in my ears, speak there
Of God's love, O live air,
Of patience, penance, prayer:
World-mothering air, air wild,
Wound with thee, in thee isled,
Fold home, fast fold thy child.

38

To what serves Mortal Beauty?

To what serves mortal beauty │ — dangerous; does set danc-
ing blood — the O-seal-that-so │ feature, flung prouder form
Than Purcell tune lets tread to? │ See: it does this: keeps warm
Men's wits to the things that are; │ what good means — where a
    glance
Master more may than gaze, │ gaze out of countenance.
Those lovely lads once, wet-fresh │ windfalls of war's storm,
How then should Gregory, a father, │ have gleanèd else from swarm-
ed Rome?   But God to a nation │ dealt that day's dear chance.
  To man, that needs would worship │ block or barren stone,
Our law says: Love what are │ love's worthiest, were all known;
World's loveliest — men's selves. Self │ flashes off frame and face.
What do then? how meet beauty? │ Merely meet it; own,
Home at heart, heaven's sweet gift; │ then leave, let that alone.
Yea, wish that though, wish all, │ God's better beauty, grace.

39

(The Soldier)

Yes.   Whý do we áll, seeing of a soldier, bless him? bless
Our redcoats, our tars? Both these being, the greater part,
But frail clay, nay but foul clay.   Here it is: the heart,
Since, proud, it calls the calling manly, gives a guess
That, hopes that, makesbelieve, the men must be no less;
It fancies, feigns, deems, dears the artist after his art;
And fain will find as sterling all as all is smart,
And scarlet wear the spirit of wár thére express.

Mark Christ our King. He knows war, served this soldiering
    through;
He of all can handle a rope best.   There he bides in bliss
Now, and séeing somewhére some mán do all that man can do,

For love he leans forth, needs his neck must fall on, kiss,
And cry 'O Christ-done deed! So God-made-flesh does too:
Were I come o'er again' cries Christ 'it should be this'.

40

(Carrion Comfort)

Not, I'll not, carrion comfort, Despair, not feast on thee;
Not untwist — slack they may be — these last strands of man
In me ór, most weary, cry *I can no more.*   I can;
Can something, hope, wish day come, not choose not to be.
But ah, but O thou terrible, why wouldst thou rude on me
Thy wring-world right foot rock? lay a lionlimb against me? scan
With darksome devouring eyes my bruisèd bones? and fan,
O in turns of tempest, me heaped there; me frantic to avoid thee
    and flee?

Why? That my chaff might fly; my grain lie, sheer and clear.
Nay in all that toil, that coil, since (seems) I kissed the rod,
Hand rather, my heart lo! lapped strength, stole joy, would laugh,
    chéer.
Cheer whom though? the hero whose heaven-handling flung me,
    fóot tród
Me? or me that fought him? O which one? is it each one? That
    night, that year
Of now done darkness I wretch lay wrestling with (my God!) my
    God.

41

No worst, there is none.   Pitched past pitch of grief,
More pangs will, schooled at forepangs, wilder wring.
Comforter, where, where is your comforting?
Mary, mother of us, where is your relief?
My cries heave, herds-long; huddle in a main, a chief
Woe, world-sorrow; on an age-old anvil wince and sing —

Then lull, then leave off. Fury had shrieked 'No ling-
ering! Let me be fell: force I must be brief'.

  O the mind, mind has mountains; cliffs of fall
Frightful, sheer, no-man-fathomed. Hold them cheap
May who ne'er hung there. Nor does long our small
Durance deal with that steep or deep. Here! creep,
Wretch, under a comfort serves in a whirlwind: all
Life death does end and each day dies with sleep.

42

Tom's Garland:*

upon the Unemployed

Tom — garlanded with squat and surly steel
Tom; then Tom's fallowbootfellow piles pick
By him and rips out rockfire homeforth — sturdy Dick;
Tom Heart-at-ease, Tom Navvy: he is all for his meal
Sure, 's bed now. Low be it: lustily he his low lot (feel
That ne'er need hunger, Tom; Tom seldom sick,
Seldomer heartsore; that treads through, prickproof, thick
Thousands of thorns, thoughts) swings though. Commonweal
Little I reck ho! lacklevel in, if all had bread:
What! Country is honour enough in all us — lordly head,
With heaven's lights high hung round, or, mother-ground
That mammocks, mighty foot. But no way sped,
Nor mind nor mainstrength; gold go garlanded
With, perilous, O nó; nor yet plod safe shod sound;
             Undenizened, beyond bound
Of earth's glory, earth's ease, all; no one, nowhere,
In wide the world's weal; rare gold, bold steel, bare
            In both; care, but share care —
This, by Despair, bred Hangdog dull; by Rage,
Manwolf, worse; and their packs infest the age.

43

Harry Ploughman

Hard as hurdle arms, with a broth of goldish flue
Breathed round; the rack of ribs; the scooped flank; lank
Rope-over thigh; knee-nave; and barrelled shank—
          Head and foot, shoulder and shank—
By a grey eye's heed steered well, one crew, fall to;
Stand at stress. Each limb's barrowy brawn, his thew
That onewhere curded, onewhere sucked or sank—
          Soared or sank—,
Though as a beechbole firm, finds his, as at a roll-call, rank
And features, in flesh, what deed he each must do—
          His sinew-service where do.

He leans to it, Harry bends, look. Back, elbow, and liquid waist
In him, all quail to the wallowing o' the plough: 's cheek crimsons;
          curls
Wag or crossbridle, in a wind lifted, windlaced—
          See his wind- lilylocks -laced;*
Churlsgrace, too, child of Amansstrength, how it hangs or hurls
Them—broad in bluff hide his frowning feet lashed! raced
With, along them, cragiron under and cold furls—
          With-a-fountain's shining-shot furls.

44

To seem the stranger lies my lot, my life
Among strangers. Father and mother dear,
Brothers and sisters are in Christ not near
And he my peace my parting, sword and strife.
    England, whose honour O all my heart woos, wife
To my creating thought, would neither hear
Me, were I pleading, plead nor do I: I wear-
y of idle a being but by where wars are rife.

I am in Ireland now; now I am at a thírd
Remove. Not but in all removes I can
Kind love both give and get. Only what word

Wisest my heart breeds dark heaven's baffling ban
Bars or hell's spell thwarts. This to hoard unheard,
Heard unheeded, leaves me a lonely began.

45

I wake and feel the fell of dark, not day.
What hours, O what black hoürs we have spent
This night! what sights you, heart, saw; ways you went!
And more must, in yet longer light's delay.
    With witness I speak this. But where I say
Hours I mean years, mean life. And my lament
Is cries countless, cries like dead letters sent
To dearest him that lives alas! away.

    I am gall, I am heartburn. God's most deep decree
Bitter would have me taste: my taste was me;
Bones built in me, flesh filled, blood brimmed the curse.
    Selfyeast of spirit a dull dough sours. I see
The lost are like this, and their scourge to be
As I am mine, their sweating selves; but worse.

46

Patience, hard thing! the hard thing but to pray,
But bid for, Patience is! Patience who asks
Wants war, wants wounds; weary his times, his tasks;
To do without, take tosses, and obey.
    Rare patience roots in these, and, these away,
Nowhere. Natural heart's ivy, Patience masks
Our ruins of wrecked past purpose. There she basks
Purple eyes and seas of liquid leaves all day.

    We hear our hearts grate on themselves: it kills
To bruise them dearer. Yet the rebellious wills
Of us we do bid God bend to him even so.
    And where is he who more and more distils
Delicious kindness? — He is patient. Patience fills
His crisp combs, and that comes those ways we know.

47

My own heart let me more have pity on; let
Me live to my sad self hereafter kind,
Charitable; not live this tormented mind
With this tormented mind tormenting yet.
    I cast for comfort I can no more get
By groping round my comfortless, than blind
Eyes in their dark can day or thirst can find
Thirst's all-in-all in all a world of wet.

Soul, self; come, poor Jackself, I do advise
You, jaded, let be; call off thoughts awhile
Elsewhere; leave comfort root-room; let joy size
At God knows when to God knows what; whose smile
's not wrung, see you; unforeseen times rather — as skies
Betweenpie mountains — lights a lovely mile.*

48

That Nature is a Heraclitean Fire and of the comfort of the Resurrection*

Cloud-puffball, torn tufts, tossed pillows | flaunt forth, then chevy
    on an air-
built thoroughfare: heaven-roysterers, in gay-gangs | they throng;
    they glitter in marches.
Down roughcast, down dazzling whitewash, | wherever an elm
    arches,
Shivelights and shadowtackle in long | lashes lace, lance, and pair.
Delightfully the bright wind boisterous | ropes, wrestles, beats earth
    bare
Of yestertempest's creases; in pool and rut peel parches
Squandering ooze to squeezed | dough, crust, dust; stanches,
    starches
Squadroned masks and manmarks | treadmire toil there
Footfretted in it.   Million-fuelèd, | nature's bonfire burns on.

But quench her bonniest, dearest | to her, her clearest-selvèd spark
Man, how fast his firedint, | his mark on mind, is gone!
Both are in an unfathomable, all is in an enormous dark
Drowned. O pity and indig | nation! Manshape, that shone
Sheer off, disseveral, a star, | death blots black out; nor mark
        Is any of him at all so stark
But vastness blurs and time | beats level. Enough! the Resurrection,
A heart's-clarion! Away grief's gasping, | joyless days, dejection.
      Across my foundering deck shone
A beacon, an eternal beam. | Flesh fade, and mortal trash
Fall to the residuary worm; | world's wildfire, leave but ash:
      In a flash, at a trumpet crash,
I am all at once what Christ is, | since he was what I am, and
This Jack, joke, poor potsherd, | patch, matchwood, immortal
   diamond,
      Is immortal diamond.

49

In honour of

St. Alphonsus Rodriguez

Laybrother of the Society of Jesus

Honour is flashed off exploit, so we say;
And those strokes once that gashed flesh or galled shield
Should tongue that time now, trumpet now that field,
And, on the fighter, forge his glorious day.
On Christ they do and on the martyr may;
But be the war within, the brand we wield
Unseen, the heroic breast not outward-steeled,
Earth hears no hurtle then from fiercest fray.

   Yet God (that hews mountain and continent,
Earth, all, out; who, with trickling increment,
Veins violets and tall trees makes more and more)
Could crowd career with conquest while there went
Those years and years by of world without event
That in Majorca Alfonso watched the door.

50

*Justus quidem tu es, Domine, si disputem tecum: verumtamen justa
loquar ad te: Quare via impiorum prosperatur? &c.*

Thou art indeed just, Lord, if I contend
With thee; but, sir, so what I plead is just.
Why do sinners' ways prosper? and why must
Disappointment all I endeavour end?
    Wert thou my enemy, O thou my friend,
How wouldst thou worse, I wonder, than thou dost
Defeat, thwart me? Oh, the sots and thralls of lust
Do in spare hours more thrive than I that spend,
Sir, life upon thy cause. See, banks and brakes
Now, leavèd how thick! lacèd they are again
With fretty chervil, look, and fresh wind shakes
Them; birds build—but not I build; no, but strain,
Time's eunuch, and not breed one work that wakes.
Mine, O thou lord of life, send my roots rain.

51

To R. B.

The fine delight that fathers thought; the strong
Spur, live and lancing like the blowpipe flame,
Breathes once and, quenchèd faster than it came,
Leaves yet the mind a mother of immortal song.
Nine months she then, nay years, nine years she long
Within her wears, bears, cares and moulds the same:
The widow of an insight lost she lives, with aim
Now known and hand at work now never wrong.
    Sweet fire the sire of muse, my soul needs this;
I want the one rapture of an inspiration.
O then if in my lagging lines you miss
The roll, the rise, the carol, the creation,
My winter world, that scarcely breathes that bliss
Now, yields you, with some sighs, our explanation.

Explanatory Notes

The numbers are those of the poems in the present volume.

1. **For a Picture of St. Dorothea.** *St. Dorothea:* martyred ca. 311 A.D. After being tortured and decapitated during the persecutions of Diocletian, she is said to have sent roses and apples to Theophilus, an administrator present at her martyrdom who, witnessing her death, jestingly asked her to do so. Seeing this miracle, he was converted, and later tortured and decapitated.

3. **The Habit of Perfection.** The last two lines, cf. Matthew 6:28: "And why take ye thought for raiment? Consider the lilies of the field, how they grow; they toil not, and neither do they spin."

4. **The Wreck of the Deutschland.**
Stanza 14, *Kentish Knock:* a sandbar in the Thames estuary.
Stanza 20, *Gertrude . . . town:* St. Gertrude the Great, a thirteenth-century mystic, and Martin Luther both hail from the town of Eisleben, Germany.
Stanza 23: *father Francis:* St. Francis, founder of the Franciscan Order, who received the five wounds of the stigmata.
Stanza 28, *Ipse:* He himself.
Stanza 29, *single eye:* Luke 11:34: "The light of the body is the eye: therefore when *thine eye* is single, thy whole body also is full of light; but when *thine eye* is evil, thy body also *is* full of darkness."

20. **Duns Scotus's Oxford.** Johannes Duns Scotus was a Medieval Scholastic philosopher and theologian. Influential both as a philosopher and a Catholic thinker, Scotus was an early champion of the doctrine of the Immaculate Conception; he also said that individuality and compassionate love were better virtues than intellection and the attainment of knowledge. Having begun his career at Oxford, he took his teaching to the University of Paris around 1313. Scotus taught a world-embracing worship of God, who was evident everywhere in the physical world. His strong, intelligent Catholicism, his deep reverence for the natural world and, perhaps most importantly, his theory of intuituve cognition (which corresponds to Hopkins' own ideas of "inscape" and "instress") made a profound impression on the poet. His influence can be seen throughout the poems (particularly in such as "Spring and Fall," "Pied Beauty" and "As kingfishers catch fire, dragonflies dráw fláme").

21. **Henry Purcell.** *Purcell* (1659–1695), the great English composer, called "England's Orpheus."
Line 1, *Have fair fallen:* "have . . . fallen" is a hortatory in the perfect tense. The sense is: "be you in a state of having fallen . . ." See also the next to last stanza of "The Loss of the Eurydice."

26. **The Candle Indoors.** *There/ . . .:* the oblique slash denotes a pause after the enjambment of "There," and also gives space and stress to "God."
Line 12, *Are you beam-blind . . . .:* Matthew 7:3–5: "And why beholdest thou the mote that is in thy brother's eye, but considerest not the beam that is in thine own eye. Or how wilt thou say to thy brother, Let me pull out the mote out of

thine eye; and, behold, a beam *is* in thine own eye. Thou hypocrite, first cast out the beam out of thine own eye; and then shalt thou see clearly to cast out the mote out of thy brother's eye."

Line 14, *spendsavour salt:* Matthew 5:13: "Ye are the salt of the earth: but if the salt have lost his savour, wherewith shall it be salted? it is thenceforth good for nothing, but to be cast out, and to be trodden under foot of men."

32. **Spelt from Sibyl's Leaves.** *Title:* cf. the "Dies irae" of the Catholic mass for the dead: "As David and the Sybil testify . . . what terror shall affright the soul when the judge comes." Also, Sibyl in classical literature is the oracle of Apollo who, when possessed by the god, trembles and drops leaves on which are written the fortunes of those consulting her (cf. Virgil's *Aeneid,* book VI).
    Line 6, *throughther:* "through-other" (Scots dialect).

36. **The Leaden Echo and the Golden Echo.** This poem is part of an unfinished verse drama set in ancient Wales. *St. Winefred:* a legendary Welsh saint of the seventh century A.D. When a chieftain cut off Winefred's head, a stream appeared where it touched the ground. This became "St. Winefred's Well" (in Flintshire, North Wales). According to the legend, Winefred's head was re-united to her body and she became the abbess of Gwytherin.

42. **Tom's Garland.** The form of this poem derives from Milton's satirical piece "On the New Forcers of Conscience Under the Long Parliament" (1646). It is called a "caudated," or tailed, sonnet, having five or six more lines or half-lines than the usual fourteen. The next poem "Harry Ploughman" is also a caudated sonnet.

43. **Harry Ploughman.** *wind- his lilylocks -laced:* his lilylocks wind-laced.

47. '**My own heart let me have more pity on;** let.' *betweenpie:* a Hopkins coinage: a verb meaning, roughly, "to color in half-shades, or colors such as those prevailing in the natural light between day and night."

48. **That Nature is a Heraclitean Fire and of the comfort of the Resurrection.** The ancient Greek philosopher Herakleitos (c. 560–480 B.C.) speculated that the physical universe (of which the soul was a part) was composed of fire, which, by variously promoting the changes that produce and destroy life, showed, by its very instability, divine properties: "This world . . . ever was and is and ever shall be an eternal living Fire, kindled and extinguished measure for measure." *Fragment 30*). As well, he believed that all things were defined by their opposites, and that the eternal "strife" occurring between them was the earthly manifestation of God ("God is day and night, summer and winter, war and peace, repletion and hunger." *Fragment 67*). Note the frequent fire imagery in Hopkins' poetry in general.

Index of Titles and First Lines

The numbers are those of pages in the present edition.